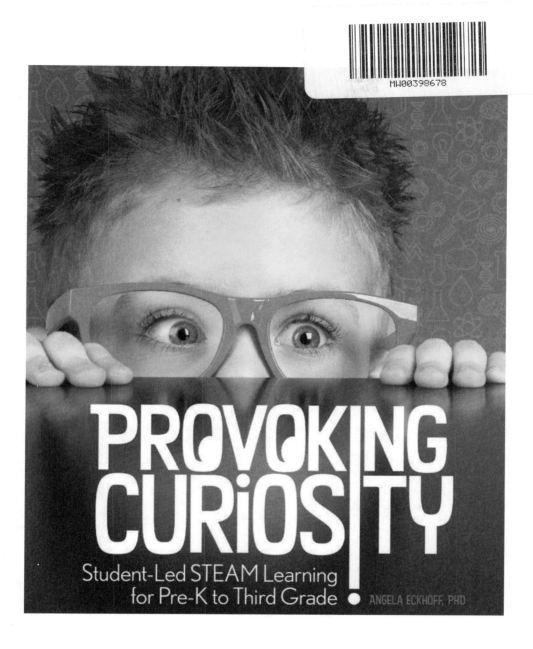

PROVOKING CURIOSITY

Student-Led STEAM Learning
for Pre-K to Third Grade

ANGELA ECKHOFF, PHD

by Angela Eckhoff, PhD

Gryphon House
www.gryphonhouse.com

LIBRARY OF CONGRESS CATALOGING-IN-PUBLICATION DATA
Library of Congress Control Number:2019953945.

BULK PURCHASE

Gryphon House books are available for special premiums and sales promotions, as well as for fund-raising use. Special editions or book excerpts also can be created to specifications. For details, call 800.638.0928.

DISCLAIMER

Gryphon House, Inc., cannot be held responsible for damage, mishap, or injury incurred during the use of or because of activities in this book. Appropriate and reasonable caution and adult supervision of children involved in activities and corresponding to the age and capability of each child involved are recommended at all times. Do not leave children unattended at any time. Observe safety and caution at all times.

Provoking Curiosity

CONTENTS

Provoking Curiosity

INTRODUCTION

PLANNING FOR STEAM PROVOCATIONS: INDEPENDENT INQUIRY AND DESIGN IN THE CLASSROOM

The best lesson plan designed by the most experienced teacher is no match for a child who decides not to engage in the act of learning. One of the first lessons I learned as a new teacher was that no matter how exciting my planned lessons were, I could not make a child learn. I could provide an interesting experience full of engaging content and hands-on materials, but the cognitive act of learning was under each child's control. Our minds are our own, and, therefore, children control what they choose to focus on, what they seek to better understand, and, ultimately, what they learn. True learning requires intention and energy on the part of the learner. No amount of telling by a teacher will support the development of new understandings for a child who is not interested.

> This book offers child-centered STEAM provocations that you can use daily in your classroom during short segments of less-structured time.

This means that we, as educators, must devote our energies and efforts to developing learning experiences that inspire children to expand their understanding of the world. We know that to build knowledge, children must be interested in a particular content idea and must also see it as relevant to their own lives. As teachers, we play a central role in the development of children's thinking as we work to offer learning experiences and classroom environments that invite and encourage young learners to engage their minds and bodies in a quest to understand.

In spite of decades of research telling us that the mind grows through playful engagement within a supportive environment, the policies guiding early childhood and primary-grades classrooms in many schools require that teachers move through content quickly in a one-size-fits-all approach. This approach often relies upon paced curricula and prescriptive approaches to content delivery that ignore ideas of engagement through playful learning and learning through play. Often, in these same classrooms, young children spend the majority of the day focused on literacy skill development with less time for science, technology, engineering, the arts, and mathematics (STEAM). STEAM learning experiences are important to incorporate daily for young children because these activities can introduce them to new ways of thinking and can connect to their personal interests and prior knowledge.

Many teachers I've worked with over the course of my career have approached me with concerns over a lack of time to include daily STEAM experiences in their classrooms. They know that the STEAM disciplines are important, and they desperately want to find ways to meet children's needs while still meeting requirements for early literacy skill development. This book offers a child-centered solution to that challenge—STEAM provocations that you can use regularly in your classroom during short segments of less-structured time.

In an interview titled "Play and the Hundred Languages of Children," published in the *American Journal of Play*, Reggio expert Lella Gandini explains that the term *provocations* describes activities that do not have a predetermined outcome or a singular objective. Instead, provocations encourage children to explore materials, interactions, ideas, and ways of thinking. Provocations can take place in all areas of your classroom or can be set up at children's workspaces. During these activities, children can work individually, with partners, or in small groups. STEAM provocations can involve materials that children can use without an adult's constant assistance. These materials encourage children to use inquiry skills, design thinking, and creativity skills.

> **Provocation:** child-driven exploration or interaction that encourages new ideas, connections, and ways of thinking

You can use the provocations in this book numerous times over the course of several days or longer as children gain experience and think through their original ideas and understandings. For young children, repetition is an important part of building new understandings and developing skills. You do not need to offer new provocation experiences each day. Observe your students, and rotate provocations or introduce new ones when the children indicate that they are ready for a change. Whether you choose one provocation for the class to complete together or you offer multiple provocations during the times of the day when you need your students to engage in thinking, exploring, and wondering, each provocation presented in this book connects to core ideas in the STEAM disciplines, centers on the development of higher-level thinking skills, and uses materials readily available in early childhood classrooms. The following are a just a few ways you can use STEAM provocations in your classroom:

- As a jump-start to the morning, with children working at tables or in centers

- As a midday experience to provide children a chance to decompress and reenergize

- As an alternative option for children who complete assigned classroom work early

- As an end-of-day experience to empower children to build their collaboration and communication skills before heading home

- As a transition time between the busier times of day, such as lunch or recess, and planned classroom work times

- As an incentive for students to build engagement throughout the day

- As an approach to remind children that learning can be enjoyable and that they can experience a variety of successes in the STEAM disciplines

UNDERSTANDiNG INDEPENDENT EXPLORAtiONS

One source of inspiration for this book comes from the world of museums. Science, art, history, and children's museums all create exhibit spaces that aim to draw in visitors for short-term, investigatory experiences featuring specific content information. These exhibits are created to engage visitors of all ages and backgrounds and, ultimately, to introduce them to a new experience that empowers them to build understanding while they explore on their own or with others at the exhibit. These experiences are referred to as *informal learning experiences* because they take place outside a school environment and are not teacher directed but are based upon specific learning objectives. The following vignette shares the experiences of two boys engaged in an informal learning experience.

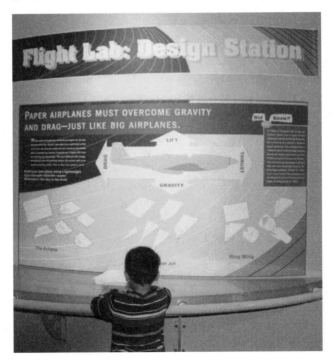

Flight Lab at the Virginia Air and Space Center

On the second floor of the Virginia Air and Space Center, Marcus and Cameron make their way to the front of the *Flight Lab: Design Station* exhibit. "Yes! We can make paper airplanes!" exclaims Marcus as he takes a sheet of paper from a stack sitting on the ledge of the exhibit.

"Which one are you going to make?" asks Cameron.

Both boys stop talking for a minute as they read and examine the possible designs suggested on the exhibit signage. Marcus, borrowing words from the exhibit's descriptive text he has just read, announces that he will make the eclipse glider because it has bigger wings "for lift." Cameron sets out to fold the jet because he is interested in speed.

As Cameron and Marcus work, they occasionally glance back at the images on the exhibit wall that detail the folds needed for each step of creating their airplanes. Once finished, the boys take their planes over to the section of the exhibit designated for test flights. Each boy takes a turn flying his airplane to see which one goes the farthest. Cameron's jet glides down over the length of the flight space as Marcus cheers it on.

Flight Lab exhibit layout at the Virginia Air and Space Center

Marcus's and Cameron's interactions with *Flight Lab* illustrate how an informal learning experience can serve to build knowledge and promote children's understandings as they explore independently. *Flight Lab* strategically combines text and visual images to invite and engage learners of all ages and literacy levels. The text and images help to scaffold children's experiences and create a space where they can work independently or alongside an adult or peer. *Flight Lab* also purposefully uses the exhibit space to both invite and structure visitors' physical interactions with the materials. The paper for visitors' airplanes is stacked neatly on a low shelf, providing ample space for people to work while positioned in front of the visual display with examples of paper-airplane folding techniques. An area for testing the flight capabilities of folded planes is located off to the side of the exhibit, providing clearly delineated spaces for folding and flight. This organization helps the visitor understand which actions are appropriate and expected in each area of the exhibit. Everything a visitor needs to know and use is intentionally positioned within the exhibit.

As early educators, we can use hands-on exhibit design to inspire similar independent-investigation opportunities in our classrooms. Intentionally designed learning spaces for young children can be engaging, informative, and enjoyable, whether the space is within a school, child-care setting, or museum. The STEAM provocations in this book invite you to create opportunities for independent explorations in which children can investigate and create, just as *Flight Lab* does.

THE ROLE OF THE ENVIRONMENT iN LEARNiNG

Within the field of early childhood education, contemporary ideas about early learning spaces are influenced in many ways by the seminal writings of early educators, theorists, and philosophers, including Maria Montessori, John Dewey, Lev Vygotsky, and Loris Malaguzzi. These influential thinkers shared a common understanding about children's learning: they all believed that children actively construct their knowledge and understanding of the world through their everyday experiences and interactions. As educators, we can weave together ideas from these influential writings to develop our own ideas of schools and classrooms as both physical and theoretical spaces where children can engage with others to build social and intrapersonal understanding, creative- and critical-thinking skills, content-knowledge understanding, communication and literacy skills, and motor skills. Every learning environment differs in the extent to which children engage in opportunities to develop these diverse skill sets, but it is important for early childhood educators to understand that environment itself plays a critical role in the types of opportunities children have to play, explore, create, and investigate.

As noted in her books *The Absorbent Mind* and *The Discovery of the Child*, Maria Montessori is widely credited with introducing educators to the importance of creating a welcoming environment for children with child-sized furnishings. She is also credited with creating learning materials based upon her knowledge of children's development, natural curiosity, and interests. Having accessible materials and furnishings within a classroom promotes children's independent access to learning materials and provides opportunities for them to explore their environment at their own pace. In her writings, Montessori stresses that the learning environment should not overwhelm children with colors, textures, or excess materials. Rather, spaces for learning should feel orderly and welcoming.

To extend the idea of child-sized and child-centered learning materials, we can draw upon ideas from the Reggio Emilia approach to early learning. In "Play and the Hundred Languages of Children," Lella Gandini notes that the idea of learning provocations was introduced to the early childhood community by Loris Malaguzzi and scholars from Reggio Emilia, Italy, after World War II. The careful treatment that Reggio educators devote to their classrooms alerts us to the possibilities the environment holds for supporting and shaping the ideas, questions, and understandings of many different types of learners.

> In a first-grade classroom, students who finish assigned work before their classmates are encouraged to choose a STEAM learning experience to explore on their own. For the past week, the class has focused on earth science, learning about different types of weather and the characteristics of each type.
>
> Levi has chosen to spend time on an arts-based science provocation. The teacher has placed several easels and sets of liquid watercolors near the classroom windows to encourage the students to think about the connections between the outdoors, the weather, and the arts. The paints are in clear jars and carefully lined up along the window's edge to allow the light to shine through them. Each color has its own paintbrush, and paper is stacked neatly beside the paint on a low table that all students can access. A sign next to the materials provides a provocation-invitation question: "Can you paint the weather?"

Watercolor paints for science explorations

Levi attaches his paper under the clip at the top of an easel and selects several jars of paint to place within the ledge at the bottom of the easel. Once his materials are in place, he moves a low stool in front of his easel, sits down, and glances out the window. The window faces the small flower garden on the school grounds. As Levi looks out the window and back to his blank paper, he begins to paint a bright, blue skyline reflective of the warm, sunny scene in the flower garden just outside.

Levi spends about ten minutes painting alongside a peer before their teacher announces that it is time to move on to the next class experience. Levi places his painting on a nearby shelf to dry, knowing that he can resume his work during his next opportunity to be inspired by the scene outside the window.

Painting the weather

GUiDED REFLECTiON

- What elements of Montessori's emphasis on accessible, child-sized materials can you find in Levi's classroom?

- What is the content emphasis of the Reggio-inspired provocation activity in this example?

- How does the teacher's placement of materials and furniture help to support the students' independence as they work within this learning center?

- Where can you find evidence of Levi's independent thinking and exploration during the experience?

EXPERiENTiAL LEARNiNG

Beginning with the provocation question, Levi connected his understandings of weather to his immediate surroundings and used his senses to visually explore his ideas. Over a century ago, John Dewey, an American philosopher, wrote in support of this kind of *experiential learning* in his books *The Child and the Curriculum*, *Democracy and Education*, and *Experience and Education*. Experiential-learning opportunities can include the elements of student reflection, child initiative, student decision making, and responsibility. Dewey's writings underscore a philosophy of education in which learning is seen as an active process started by students themselves, as opposed to something that is done to children. In other words, learning is an experience that children initiate and sustain through their intentions and interactions, not a process in which teachers deliver knowledge to students through scripted instruction. Dewey argues that supportive educational experiences should engage, excite, foster curiosity, and, perhaps most importantly, inspire a desire to persist with learning. Contemporary extensions of Dewey's ideas appear in experiential learning theory, which—as educational theorist David Kolb explains in his book *Experiential Learning*—highlights the central role of experience in the process of learning.

Placing a primary importance on experience in learning brings to the forefront the child and understandings of playful, engaging learning. Early learning environments that hold experiential learning as a core philosophy provide young children with opportunities to choose what, when, and how to engage and learn within an environment specifically designed to embody playful learning experiences. The pedagogical beliefs and practices guiding early learning programs and primary-grade classrooms vary based upon the educational philosophies and beliefs about learning held by the individuals at each particular site. However, a child-driven approach typically emphasizes educational philosophies and practices that address the needs of the whole child and embrace the diverse abilities of all children.

OBJECT-CENTERED LEARNiNG

Object-centered learning is another important element in understanding the role of the environment in learning. Within an object-centered approach, learners actively construct meaning during their interactions with objects that they can view or touch. Object-centered learning can support the development of many cognitive skills—such as observation, questioning, and prediction—and it allows children to use many of their senses as they explore. As researchers Ingrid Pramling Samuelsson, Sonja Sheridan, and Pia Williams point out in their article "Five Preschool Curricula—Comparative Perspective," an important tenet of Reggio Emilia philosophy is encouraging the child to develop individual understandings of the world and the objects within their world. According to the book *In the Spirit of the Studio*, edited by Lella Gandini and colleagues, Reggio Emilia educators encourage students to interact with a variety of natural and manmade objects and to use them to create meaning, explore, and communicate their understandings. Engaging in hands-on, minds-on explorations of objects helps to provide us with new information which, in turn, helps us to develop new ideas and understandings. A model of an airplane can show us the many external components of planes but also can help us to think about how planes move through the sky.

In his book *Thought and Language*, influential scholar and psychologist Lev Vygotsky writes of the significance of cultural artifacts, or objects, in the processes of learning for all learners. Vygotsky stresses that cultural meanings are embedded within both objects and language. Just as we can learn from stories, books, and poems, we can also learn from blocks, artworks, or digital technologies. The objects that teachers place within early learning classrooms for visual and physical exploration work to shape the types of learning interactions that take place, as well as the content of that learning. Intentionally selected objects and materials for student exploration, building, construction, deconstruction, and modification are key to the provocations described throughout this book.

PUTTiNG THEORY iNTO PRACTiCE

The theoretical ideas behind experiential learning and provocations and the role of objects in learning will help you to design a learning environment for your students that promotes the development of inquiry and creativity skills. Such environments view young children as competent, capable learners and provide the space for children to investigate and explore at their own pace. Teachers in these environments work to guide, facilitate, and collaborate with children as they engage in minds-on, hands-on explorations to develop their understandings.

Learning environments capable of supporting provocation experiences include these hallmarks:

- Opportunities to explore based on learner interests

- Opportunities for active discovery, construction of meaning, or both

- Student-led activities

- Exploration of real-world objects and tools for learning

- Collaboration between a student, his peers, and their teachers

These hallmarks form a foundation on which children can build knowledge and skills using the STEAM provocation experiences described throughout this book.

HOW THiS BOOK SUPPORTS INQUiRY- AND DESiGN-BASED LEARNiNG AND CREATiVE THiNKiNG

INQUiRY-BASED LEARNiNG

Inquiry-based learning can play a central role in the development of meaningful learning opportunities as children explore STEAM content. During inquiry-based learning experiences, teachers act as guides to support children by asking questions and designing rich, engaging opportunities for exploration. Inquiry-based learning involves opportunities for children to engage in the topic or challenge, explore using materials and media, explain their thinking, and elaborate upon their ideas. In their report *The BSCS 5E Instructional Model*, researchers Rodger Bybee and colleagues note that, during inquiry experiences, children also have opportunities to evaluate their new ideas and constructions as they develop solutions and observe new outcomes.

Inquiry-based learning requires these process skills: observing, exploring, questioning, making predictions, using simple tools and technologies, and conducting simple investigations. The STEAM provocations in this book all begin by posing a question to prompt children's interest and to encourage them to engage in questioning, exploration, and creation.

DESiGN-BASED LEARNiNG

Like inquiry-based learning, design-based learning is a constructivist learning approach in which students are actively involved in the process of discovery learning. Design-based approaches to learning in early childhood classrooms recognize that young children learn in a "just-in-time" manner (that is, right before they need to use the content or skill) while taking the next steps in the learning process. Essentially, design-based experiences are authentic and hands on, have clearly defined outcomes that allow for multiple solution pathways, and promote student-centered work.

In this book, the engineering-design and visual arts provocations include familiar and easy-to-work-with materials and encourage multiple design iterations so children can improve and refine their ideas and work. The provocations involve loosely structured problem-solving tasks that are open ended and have no one correct pathway to a solution.

As in inquiry-based learning, during design-based experiences, teachers play a critical role by offering support and encouragement throughout the cycles of problem exploration and solution finding. In this role, teachers can supply children with needed materials, provide time and space for exploration, and scaffold student thinking through close observation and open-ended questioning.

CREATIVE THINKING

Inquiry- and design-based learning involve many opportunities for children to think creatively. Creative-thinking skills are essential for children to develop in early childhood, and STEAM provocations offer another opportunity to support and extend this facet of children's development. Creative thinking is part of the learning process involving exploration and discovery and encourages social interaction and promotes individual ownership of ideas. When young children have opportunities to engage with challenging, reflective learning experiences, they build both creative- and critical-thinking skills.

Creative-thinking skills used during STEAM provocations include the following:

- **Visualization:** seeing past problems to find solutions

- **Communication and collaboration:** talking with others about ideas

- **Solution finding:** developing new ideas and ways to solve problems

- **Fluency:** thinking accurately and quickly in the face of challenges

- **Flexibility:** adjusting thinking from old ideas to new ones

- **Elaboration:** explaining ideas, problems, and challenges with greater detail

- **Originality:** developing new ideas and outcomes

- **Problem solving:** creating solutions to challenges

- **Strategic planning:** thinking ahead and developing a plan for approaching a challenge

In Marta's first-grade class, she is working alongside her three tablemates to build a car that will move the fastest in a whole-class race, which will use small ramps later in the day during science time. The class has been exploring force and motion this week. They have access to a variety of child-friendly building materials to create their cars. Marta's table has decided that they want to build a small car so it is light and can go fast, but they are debating whether to use large or small wheels. As the children discuss that "big wheels move faster" and "the small wheels will fit the car," Marta suggests that they build two small cars: one with big wheels and one with small wheels. Once built, the group can test the cars' speeds at their own table before the big race at the end of the day. Marta's tablemates agree and set to work in teams to hurriedly build their two test cars.

Allowing your students opportunities to work through challenges during student-led explorations, such as those encountered by Marta's tablemates, encourages them to build both content understandings and communication and collaboration skills. These skills are quite valuable for young learners. Time spent exploring and questioning with peers provides naturally occurring opportunities to experience new ways of working and learning together.

CREATiNG PROVOCATiON EXPERiENCES iN YOUR CLASSROOM

The STEAM provocations described in the chapters that follow are intended to be used flexibly in your classroom. The idea is to find times throughout your day—such as in the morning to welcome students, as your class transitions from one part of the day to another, in the spare time created when children finish lessons early, or even at the end of the day to give children time to decompress and engage with each other—when you can provide the space and time for children to explore, investigate, plan, and create. The provocations in this book are intended for children working independently or in small groups with limited need for direct teacher attention. The experiences are also intended to build skills in inquiry, design, and creative thinking, so remember that the products the children create are not of central importance; the processes they go through during the provocation are the most valuable outcome.

Throughout this book, you will note that the materials suggested for use in the provocations may include specific materials that might be new to your students or a material or tool your students haven't previously used. In such cases, you will need to take into account your students' ages and developmental levels, state or school requirements, and your personal comfort level with the material. You can certainly substitute a material you feel is more appropriate for any provocation in this text. It is also important to introduce all materials prior to student use and to discuss your expectations for their use. Guidelines specific to a particular material or tool will help your students learn to use materials safely and appropriately. Because children will work with many types of materials during the provocations in this book, the following suggestions will help you to organize your classroom and prepare your students for these investigations.

- Share and discuss your expectations with the children so they understand how to respect and use materials carefully.

- Introduce any new materials prior to including them in a provocation experience so that children are familiar with how they can be used.

- Carefully organize the provocation materials so that the children can help keep the materials organized after use—tabletop bins help to keep materials organized and in one place.

- Ensure that children understand that they can work on a provocation for many days. Repeated explorations give them the time necessary to build their skills and understandings. If you choose not to have a permanent center for exploration, you can easily rotate provocation materials in and out when time allows. Along with tabletop bins, large shallow trays can be used to hold children's in-progress works for later use.

- Children's independent work can sometimes result in messiness, but remember, the mess is a temporary challenge. Encourage children to clean and organize their workspaces prior to moving on from a provocation. Taking care of their own materials and space builds important independence skills.

- As provocation experiences come to an end, ensure that children have opportunities to share and discuss their discoveries and creations.

As you explore and plan with the provocations in the chapters that follow, you will note that it is suggested that children are encouraged to write or draw their experiences and understandings during their explorations. Student-created documentation of their learning is important because it helps to make the experience and their ideas visible and concrete for themselves and others. Their writings and drawings can also be very helpful for you to review in order to create your own understanding of their knowledge, questions, and understandings. You can use this information to help you decide the next steps for the provocation or to move on to a new provocation experience if the children are ready. You will also note that each provocation encouraging student documentation reminds you to decide to use either paper or small dry-erase boards. Each material has different affordances: Paper is a more permanent material for student representations; a dry-erase board allows children to easily make changes without fear of writing something they think might not be correct or an idea that they are not fully comfortable with at the moment. Both materials have their value, and you should make decisions based on what will work best for your students.

PROVOCATiON QUESTiONS AND PROMPTS

As this book features experiences that are meant to be student led, you will notice that each new provocation begins with an open-ended question or prompt to encourage children to begin their explorations and investigations. This prompt can be written down and placed among the materials available for children to use in the activity if your students are able to use their literacy skills to decode and comprehend the prompt. For younger students and students needing additional reading supports, the provocation prompts can be read aloud prior to their engagement in the experience. You may also find it helpful, especially as your students are just beginning to engage in provocations, to spend time briefly discussing the provocation and inviting the students to share their initial questions or ideas. This initial discussion is also a wonderful place to talk with your students about the materials and tools available and to provide them with any guidelines or instructions related to the materials themselves. It is important to keep these initial discussions open ended to maintain a focus on the processes of learning and exploration rather than on providing students with a set of steps to complete. The goal of the provocation prompts is to encourage children's initial interests and provide them with a general line of possible inquiry.

Provoking Curiosity

CHAPTER 1

SCIENCE
PROVOCATIONS

cience provocations can be introduced to children in many ways. You can use the provocation to prompt their curiosity and explore their prior knowledge about a topic before you begin formal curricular study. You can encourage science provocations using related content ideas and materials children are experiencing simultaneously during more formal lessons. Or you can use a science provocation at the end of a unit of formal study so that your students have an opportunity to apply their new understandings and experiences. There is no one right way or time to use a particular provocation, but it is important to connect their student-led work during provocations to other experiences in your classroom.

In particular to science provocations, students are often working with a variety of materials, so you will want to take time to explain the materials that are available for them to use and also explain any restrictions for materials use that you'd like the students to follow. A brief introduction is typically all that is needed; remember to keep the experience as open ended and child led as possible, given the nature of the experience.

Provoking Curiosity

PROVOCATION 1: PHYSICAL-CHANGE COLLAGE

Physical changes are an important part of understanding the three common states of matter: solid, liquid, and gas. Physical changes can include changes in the shape or appearance of an object, such as tearing a piece of paper, dissolving sugar in water, or bending chenille stems into shapes. Physical changes do not make new substances. Because objects do not become new or different substances during a physical change, often the change can be reversed. For instance, a bent chenille pipe cleaner can be straightened.

In this provocation, children are invited to conduct physical changes with everyday objects and to create collages using the materials they have manipulated.

CONTENT AND SKILLS EXPERIENCED IN THIS PROVOCATION

- **Physical science:** study of matter and physical change

- **Visual arts:** collage work

- **Creativity skills:** visualization, originality, strategic planning

MATERIALS

- A variety of materials to alter (such as paper to tear, cut, or crumple; cardboard to bend or cut; watercolor paints to mix; chenille stems to bend; or clay to shape)

- Paper

- Scissors

- Glue or tape

PROVOCATION PROMPT

How can you change these materials to make them different than they are?

DiFFERENTiATiON BY GRADE LEVEL

- Pre-K and kindergarten students will enjoy creating changes to the materials.
  Provide them with containers to put the materials in as they rip, tear, crumple, and
  cut. The children can create an ephemeral, or temporary, collage by just laying
  out their pieces in a design on their table while working individually or in a group. A
  temporary collage can encourage them to spend more time exploring the physical
  changes in the materials without the need to create a take-away product. This way,
  they can lay down, pick up, alter, and move objects countless times.

For first-, second-, and third-graders, try encouraging them to create permanent
collages using their altered materials and to add other arts media, such as mixed-color
paints. Providing trays for children to work in will help to contain the materials and make
cleanup easier.

A second-grader's physical-change collage

PROVOCATION 2: BUILD A BUG, BUILD AN INSECT, BUILD AN ARTHROPOD

"It's a bug!" is a common phrase heard across all playgrounds as young children explore all those small creatures that walk, fly, and crawl. This provocation draws children's attention to the differences among bugs, insects, and arthropods as a means to build both life-science understandings and classification skills.

- A *bug* has a mouth shaped like a straw (called a *stylet*), no teeth, and tough forewings. Common bugs include beetles, aphids, stink bugs, and water bugs.

- An *insect* has a hard outer shell (called an *exoskeleton*), three main body parts (head, thorax, and abdomen), and usually two pairs of wings and three pairs of legs. Common insects include ants, bees, mosquitos, butterflies, and beetles.

- *Arthropods* make up about 85 percent of all known animals on Earth. They have segmented bodies, multiple jointed legs or limbs, and exoskeletons and are cold-blooded. Common arthropods are spiders, ticks, centipedes, lobsters, crabs, shrimp, and scorpions.

For this provocation, children visually explore color images or real specimens (typically encased in resin or acrylic blocks) of insects, bugs, and arthropods. To help children as they explore the differences among these creatures, it can be helpful to provide the children with images of various insects, bugs, and arthropods for them to reference.

CONTENT AND SKILLS EXPERIENCED IN THIS PROVOCATION

- **Life science:** the study of the earth's animals and the ways their bodies support movement

- **Creativity skills:** visualization, solution finding, flexibility, problem solving

MATERIALS

- Color images or real specimens of insects, bugs, and arthropods

- Various small materials, or larger materials that can be cut, to construct models (such as chenille pipe cleaners, buttons, clear counters, glass cabochons, toothpicks, and paper straws)

- Scissors (first through third grade)

- Glue or tape

- Playdough or modeling clay

- Paper and pencils (third grade)

PROVOCATION PROMPT

Can you build an insect, bug, or arthropod?

DIFFERENTIATION BY GRADE LEVEL

- Pre-K and kindergarten students benefit from working with one animal type at a time and using materials that are already cut or small enough to use immediately.

- First- and second-grade students benefit from the opportunity to choose and manipulate the materials to fit their needs, so include scissors to enable them to cut their pieces to size. Have defined spaces for children to work on their creations—trays work well if children are working individually.

- Third-grade students could expand this provocation by thinking about the ways each animal uses its various parts to survive. Include paper and pencils to encourage the children to think and write about how a butterfly uses its wings or an ant uses its legs.

A kindergartner's *Build an Insect*

PROVOCATiON 3: ROCK CLASSiFiCATiON

Rocks, and all earth materials, are a source of perpetual wonder for children as they notice how some rocks are shiny, some are rough, and others sparkle in the sunlight. There are three main types of rock—sedimentary, metamorphic, and igneous—and the differences between them have to do with how they are formed.

- *Sedimentary rock* is formed from sand, shells, pebbles, and other earth materials, which you can see in the rock. Sedimentary rock is soft and can crumble easily.

- *Metamorphic rock* is formed below the Earth's surface from the intense heat and pressure. The rocks that result from this process frequently have ribbonlike layers and may also have visible, shiny crystals.

- *Igneous rock* is formed when magma cools and hardens. Magma can cool inside the Earth or erupt onto the surface from volcanoes. When lava cools very quickly, no crystals form and the rock appears shiny and glasslike. Gas bubbles can also become trapped during the cooling process and leave behind tiny holes.

In this provocation, the children will have the opportunity to explore a variety of rocks firsthand and explore ways of grouping the rocks according to their similarities and differences.

CONTENT AND SKiLLS EXPERiENCED iN THiS PROVOCATiON

- **Earth science:** study of the Earth's materials

- **Math:** classification

- **Creativity skills:** elaboration, problem solving

MATERIALS

- Various rocks

- Magnifying glasses

- Containers for sorting (pre-K and kindergarten)

- Rock-classification sheets (first through third grade)

PROVOCATION PROMPTS

- Can you group the rocks by the way they look? (pre-K and kindergarten)

- Can you group the rocks by the way they feel? (pre-K and kindergarten)

- Can you sort the rocks by type? (first through third grade)

DIFFERENTIATION BY GRADE LEVEL

- Pre-K and kindergarten students benefit from the opportunity to explore and group rocks by categories that the children create, such as rough, smooth, round, and shiny. Consider including a small number of containers for the children to sort rocks independently or with a partner.

- First-, second-, and third-grade students benefit from a more challenging experience in which they can learn the names of the different types of rocks as well as the characteristics that make each rock type unique. In addition to providing rocks and magnifying glasses, providing the children with a classification sheet, such as the following chart, points their attention to the important characteristics that help them understand the types of rock they are exploring.

ROCK CLASSIFICATION CHART

CRYSTALS	Do you see small shiny spots like tiny mirrors on the rock?	It may be metamorphic.
SHINY SURFACE	Is the rock shiny and smooth?	It may be igneous.
RIBBON LAYERS	Are there wavy or straight lines of different colors on the rock?	It may be metamorphic.
FOSSILS	Do you see imprints of small shells, leaves, or insects in the rock?	It may be sedimentary.
BUBBLES	Can you find small holes in the rock?	It may be igneous.
SAND OR PEBBLES	Do you feel and see small pebbles or grains of sand in the rock?	It may be sedimentary.

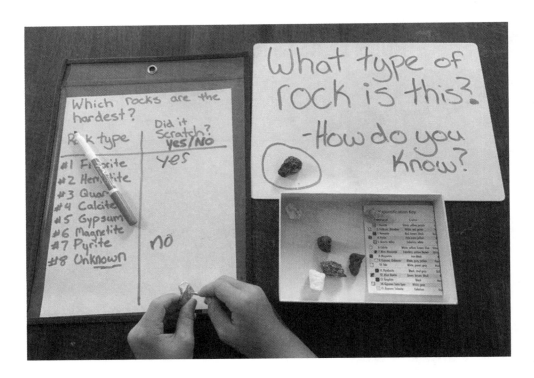

Earth materials provocation

Provoking Curiosity

PROVOCATiON 4: LiGHT SOURCES AND SHADOWS

Exploring light and shadow is an activity that young learners readily engage in, both inside and outside the classroom. There are many ideas that can be explored during a provocation experience with light: the relationship between the direction of a light source and the object being illuminated and the shadow generated, understanding that objects must be illuminated (either from an external or internal light source) in order to be seen, or the exploration of the ways that objects made with differing materials block or allow light to pass through to varying degrees (*transparent, translucent, opaque*) or that reflect light (*reflective*).

In this provocation, children will explore the interactions between a light source, the properties of an object, and shadows.

CONTENT AND SKiLLS EXPERiENCED iN THiS PROVOCATiON

- **Earth and space sciences:** study of light

- **Creativity skills:** visualization, strategic planning, communication and collaboration

MATERiALS

- A portable light source (large or small flashlights work best)

- Small objects of varying sizes

- Paper or a whiteboard

- Pencils or dry-erase markers

- Transparent, translucent, opaque, and reflective materials (second and third grades)

PROVOCATION PROMPTS

- How do light and shadows interact? (pre-K through third grade)

- How does the direction of the light source change shadows? (kindergarten and first grade)

- How does light move through objects made with different materials? (second and third grade)

DIFFERENTIATION BY GRADE LEVEL

- Pre-K students will enjoy the opportunity to explore making shadows with everyday objects. You can encourage them to use a variety of objects and even flashlights or other light sources of varying sizes to experience shadow and light differences.

- Kindergartners and first-graders can extend their exploration to exploring how the shadow changes when they shine the flashlight from above, behind, or from the sides of the object. You can also encourage them to draw or trace the shadows they create as they explore.

- For second- and third-graders, the provocation can extend to exploring how different materials allow light through, reflect light, or block light. Include transparent, translucent, opaque, and reflective materials. You can encourage students to explore the relationship between the properties of the object and the shadow being created as they explore. Inviting students to record their observations will support them as they engage with multiple types of materials by making their observations concrete.

Provoking Curiosity

PROVOCATION 5: MAGNET PLAY

Many children begin playing with magnets as young toddlers, moving magnets on the refrigerators in their homes. Their interest grows throughout childhood as they experience how magnets work in everyday items. Magnetism is a force that can *attract* (pull closer) or *repel* (push away) objects that have a magnetic material inside them. The study of magnets is an important component of understanding force, motion, and energy.

In this provocation, children explore the interactions between a variety of magnets and objects to determine the relative strength or weakness of the magnetic force.

CONTENT AND SKILLS EXPERIENCED IN THIS PROVOCATION

- **Physical science:** magnetism and force

- **Creativity skills:** visualization, solution finding

MATERIALS

- Magnets of varying sizes, including magnet wands, horseshoe magnets, or magnet chips as appropriate

- Magnets of varying strengths (first through third grade)

- Metallic objects of varying sizes

- Nonmetallic objects of varying sizes

- Small baskets or trays

- Paper or a whiteboard

- Pencils or dry-erase markers as appropriate

PROVOCATION PROMPTS

- Can you make an object move without touching it? (pre-K and kindergarten)

- What does a magnet attract or repel? (first through third grade)

- Can the magnets help you move and stack objects? (first through third grade)

DIFFERENTIATION BY GRADE LEVEL

- Pre-K and kindergarten students will enjoy the opportunity to explore moving metallic objects with magnets of varying strengths. You can encourage them to sort objects based upon each object's interactions with the magnet.

- For first-, second-, and third-graders, the provocation prompt can serve to introduce the language of magnetism: attract and repel. Encourage the children to think about the properties of the objects as they interact with a magnet. Including magnets of varying sizes and strengths will invite your students to explore the strength of the attraction. Invite students to record their observations, which will support them as they engage with multiple objects by making their observations concrete. This provocation can also be extended into a building challenge by encouraging students to think about how they could use the magnets to stack magnetic objects. You will want to ensure that the magnets available to the children in this provocation are strong enough to pick up and move small objects.

Magnet provocation

PROVOCATiON 6: BODiES iN MOVEMENT

A *body system* is a collection of parts able to work to support growth, reproduction, and survival. The skeleton provides a framework on which the human body is arranged. It is *articulated* (has joints) to allow for movement, and our skeletal muscles control that movement.

In this provocation, your students will have the opportunity to use pictures or small-scale models of the human skeleton or specific parts of the skeleton to draw their own representations. This experience encourages observational drawing, which is an important skill as children draw what they see rather than what they think an image should look like in their minds. This means that the pictures or models you provide for them are very important, as they will help to guide their drawings in a meaningful way.

CONTENT AND SKiLLS EXPERiENCED iN THiS PROVOCATiON

- **Life science:** study of the form and function of the human body

- **Physical education:** the human musculoskeletal system

- **Visual arts:** observational drawing

- **Creativity skills:** visualization, flexibility, communication through drawing

MATERiALS

- Photos or small-scale models of the human body or specific body parts
- Sketch paper or small whiteboards
- Pencils or dry-erase markers
- Large butcher paper (if available)

PROVOCATION PROMPTS

- Can you draw a hand? (pre-K and kindergarten)

- Can your hand throw a ball? (first through third grade)

- Can your arm throw a ball? (first through third grade)

- Can your body kick a ball? (first through third grade)

Because this provocation asks children to draw from observation, their drawing skills will be challenged. Dry-erase boards work well for such challenges, because children can modify their drawings by simply wiping out any mark they wish to change. If desired, you can substitute sketch paper and pencils for the dry-erase boards and markers.

DIFFERENTIATION BY GRADE LEVEL

- Pre-K and kindergarten students will benefit from simpler provocation prompts. Models or pictures of hands or other body parts will help the children use observation to create their representations rather than just drawing from memory. In addition, you can encourage them to work with partners to physically trace a hand or an entire body, if you have large butcher paper available, and to color in or decorate their drawings once the outline is completed.

- First- and second-grade students are building their abilities to draw from observation and will benefit from watching you model drawing from observation. It can also help to work alongside the children as they gain experience with observational drawing, provided you narrate your actions: "See how the finger is actually made up of three segments that move? I'm going to draw each segment of the finger separately instead of just drawing one long finger." Remember that you don't need to draw perfectly; your narrations and drawings are meant to encourage children to observe and build their skills and understanding.

- Challenge third-grade students by encouraging them to draw more detail in their sketches. Check in with them to prompt them to look for connections between the models or pictures and the movement the children detail in their drawings. This practice helps support the children in making their own connections between observation and visualization of movement.

A third-grader's body in movement

A first-grader's catching hand

PROVOCATiON 7: STRUCTURES OF LEAVES AND PLANTS

Growth and change in life science are important topics of natural interest to young children, as they see changes in plants in their everyday environments. Simple observation provocations that explore the structures of leaves and plants can provide a way to supplement and support the life-science investigations you complete as a class.

Plant structures—roots, leaves, stems, flowers, fruit, and seeds—all have different roles and contribute to a plant's ability to survive. Plant roots bring in water and *nutrients* (food) from the soil. Plant stems hold the plant upright and contain *xylem* and *phloem* (transport tissues) to deliver the water and nutrients brought in by the roots. Plant leaves absorb sunlight and exchange gases—oxygen for respiration and carbon dioxide for photosynthesis. *Photosynthesis* is a process that uses sunlight to convert carbon dioxide and water into food. Flowers are the reproductive part of most plants and contain pollen and tiny eggs called *ovules*. After pollination of the flower and fertilization of the ovule, the ovule develops into a fruit. Plant fruits provide a covering for seeds, which contain new plants.

In this provocation, your students engage in a hands-on exploration of real plants and parts of plants. While looking at images of plants and their parts in a science workbook provides children with some basic understanding of how plants grow, it is very powerful to explore an entire plant, from roots to flowers. You can strengthen this experience even more for students if you grow a flower or even grass from a seed in the classroom. This provocation encourages them to explore not only the life cycle of a plant but also the structures of the plant's parts.

CONTENT AND SKILLS EXPERIENCED IN THIS PROVOCATION

- **Life science:** study of the structure of plants

- **Visual arts:** observational drawing

- **Creativity skills:** communication through drawing, elaboration of understandings and observations

MATERIALS

- Various whole plants (including attached roots) or plant parts (leaves, flowers, seeds)

- Sketch paper

- Drawing tools with sharp points for fine lines and details (such as pencils, colored pencils, fine-tipped markers, or sharp crayons)

- Magnifying glasses

PROVOCATION PROMPTS

- Can you draw or trace this [plant part or picture of a plant part]? (pre-K and kindergarten)

- Look carefully at the plant [or plant part]. What do you see? (first through third grade)

- How do the parts of a plant work together? (third grade)

DIFFERENTIATION BY GRADE LEVEL

- Encourage pre-K and kindergarten students to trace the plant parts or even create crayon rubbings of leaves or flowers. Draw their attention to specific plant parts rather than to a whole plant in order to build their understanding of each part.

- First- and second-grade students can create detailed observational drawings of the various parts of the plant. As with the pre-K and kindergarten students, continue to present the parts independently to support focused observations.

- Third-grade students can observe and document whole plants and enjoy observing a plant out of soil in order to clearly see the roots.

A kindergartner's leaf drawing

Provoking Curiosity

CHAPTER 2

TECHNOLOGY
PROVOCATIONS

Technology can pose challenges to teachers of young children because classroom funding for technology gadgets and materials is often limited in early childhood classrooms. However, these limitations shouldn't prevent you from encouraging your students to use technology to support and extend their learning. The provocations in this chapter use both readily accessible technology, such as tablets or computers, and specific technology materials, such as simple robotics. It is best to get started right away by using the technologies you have available while you research funding possibilities for more specific tools you'd like to provide in your classroom. In addition, several of the technology provocations presented in this chapter encourage children to access the internet to explore and research. In these cases, it is important for you to preview any sites you'll be using in the classroom to ensure that the content is both appropriate and accessible for your students to navigate independently.

Provoking Curiosity

PROVOCATiON 1: EXPLORiNG THE WORLD

Some benefits of including technology in the classroom are the opportunities for children to research ideas of interest to them and to explore the world beyond their local community. For this provocation, children work in pairs or teams to research a country or locality and document their research experience.

Before using this provocation, explore the websites or apps you plan to direct the children to, in order to ensure that they are safe and appropriate for your students. Questions that will help you to evaluate possible websites or apps include the following:

- Can the children manipulate the website or app on their own or with minimal adult assistance?

- Does the content meet the needs of this provocation experience?

- Is the content at a level the children can understand?

- Is the website or app engaging and interactive?

Reliable and safe websites for children to explore the world include the following:

- National Geographic Kids: https://kids.nationalgeographic.com/explore/countries/

- World Atlas: https://www.worldatlas.com/

- Discovery Education: https://www.discoveryeducation.com/community/virtual-field-trips/

- 360 Cities: https://www.360cities.net/

- Scholastic Global Trek: http://teacher.scholastic.com/activities/globaltrek/

Research that explores children's technology use indicates that collaborative uses of technology—in which children work together as pairs or teams—best support children's communication skills and understanding of the content learned through technology explorations. This occurs as children expand each other's understanding through collaboration and conversation.

- **Technology:** use of digital tools to construct knowledge

- **Social studies:** understanding the culture and places people live in around the world

- **Creativity skills:** communication and collaboration, solution finding, elaboration

In this provocation your students will be conducting independent research alone or with peers to learn more about a place of their choosing. As most social studies experiences begin with younger children learning about the places and people closest to them, you may decide to encourage this age group to stay more local in their explorations. You can encourage older students to broaden their explorations around the globe to keep this provocation in line with the other social studies content you explore as a class.

MATERiALS

Computers or tablets

PROVOCATiON PROMPT

Where in the world will you go?

DiFFERENTiATiON BY GRADE LEVEL

- Pre-K and kindergarten students need simple websites that show videos or read content to them. You can also encourage the children to screenshot or photograph the content they learn about as part of the exploration experience. Provide time for the children to share their experiences and understandings with you or the whole class as a way to build reflection and elaboration into the experience—talking with others helps children to better understand what they have explored.

- First-, second-, and third-grade students can explore websites with more detail and may find it valuable to visit more than one website during this experience. Encourage the children to document their experiences by writing or drawing the important ideas or facts they discover. You can also extend the experience by inviting the children to spend time creating posters or books about the localities they explore.

PROVOCATION 2: A VIRTUAL ZOO TRIP: GATHERING DATA

Animals provide a natural point of interest for many young children and are an important topic within life science. To support children's interest and explorations in this provocation, you should guide their use of trusted internet sources to gather information regarding the physical characteristics, behaviors, and habitat of an animal of their choosing. Using the websites with child-friendly information on a variety of animals, such as those from your local zoo or even a larger zoo such as the San Diego Zoo (https://zoo.sandiegozoo.org/animals-plants), can provide your students with opportunities to employ research strategies to gather information, photos, and other digital resources related to their interests. This type of research experience encourages students to build their content knowledge and research skills by actively exploring real-world issues and interests.

CONTENT AND SKILLS EXPERIENCED IN THIS PROVOCATION

- **Technology:** using technological tools to gather information

- **Life science:** understanding animals, their habitats, and their actions

- **Creativity skills:** visualization, strategic planning, solution finding, and communication and collaboration

MATERIALS

- Computers or tablets

- Paper or a whiteboard

- Pencils or dry-erase markers

PROVOCATiON PROMPTS

- What does an animal (your choice) need to survive? (pre-K through third grade)

- Do animals solve problems? (first through third grades)

As noted in the provocation Exploring the World, contemporary research on digital learning suggests that children's collaborative use of technology helps to support their experience and understanding. Consider encouraging your students to work in pairs or small teams for this provocation.

DiFFERENTiATiON BY GRADE LEVEL

- As pre-K and kindergarten students have limited experience using web sources to collect information, it will help if you scaffold their interactions by preselecting an animal. Or you could help the children work together to make a group decision on their animal selection. You will need to provide access to simple websites that show videos or read content to them. The San Diego Zoo website works great for young children, as there is a lot of imagery and video content for them to explore. You can also encourage the children to screenshot or photograph the content they learn about as part of the exploration experience. Be sure to provide time for them to share their experience and understandings with you or the whole class to build reflection and elaboration into the experience. Talking with others helps children to better understand what they have explored.

- First-, second-, and third-grade students will be able to explore websites with more detail and may find it valuable to visit more than one website during this experience. As children gain more animal knowledge to build upon, the provocation can extend to exploring how different animals use their unique characteristics and skills to solve problems and adapt to their environments. Encourage the children to document their experiences by writing or drawing the important ideas or facts they discover in this experience. You can also extend the experience further by inviting the children to spend time reporting their research to their classmates.

Animal provocation

PROVOCATION 3: ROBOTS! MAKE THEM MOVE!

Digital technologies are an important part of children's lives, and supportive explorations in the classroom will help them to understand how to use technologies in fun, meaningful ways. Because many children experience passive technology use in their out-of-school lives, such as watching videos or scrolling through images, they need opportunities for active and challenging engagement with digital technologies.

Coding, also known as *computer programming*, is an important skill set for children to learn through playful engagement. Young children need exposure to coding experiences to understand and interact knowledgeably with technology. Coding involves logical planning, sequencing, and step-by-step actions. In particular, robotics coding experiences encourage children to engage in problem solving, planning, and exploring cause and effect.

In this provocation, children will engage with robots designed specifically for use with young learners. These objects are both easy to use without adult help and durable (but not indestructible). Robotics sets are a large financial investment, so make sure you explore and play with the technology yourself prior to purchasing.

Depending upon the set you choose, children can code by physically connecting elements together with modular robotics or by using a partner app to tell the robot how to move. As with all digital technologies in early childhood classrooms, encourage children to work together in pairs or small teams for this type of provocation.

CONTENT AND SKILLS EXPERIENCED IN THIS PROVOCATION

- **Technology:** use of digital tools to construct knowledge, use of design thinking to identify and solve problems

- **Creativity skills:** visualization, communication and collaboration, solution finding, flexibility, problem solving, strategic planning

MATERiALS

A digital robotics technology that supports engagement through coding (such as Cubelets, MOSS kits, Artie 3000, Dash or Dot robots from Wonder Workshop, Makeblock kits, or Lego BOOST)

PROVOCATiON PROMPT

How do robots move?

DiFFERENTiATiON BY GRADE LEVEL

- Pre-K and kindergarten students need simple modular robotics kits, such as Cubelets and MOSS kits, which essentially have children code by connecting blocks together. Young children will benefit from a simple demonstration of the robotics prior to use. Talk with them about how to use and treat these materials in the classroom so that the children explore with care.

- First-, second-, and third-grade students can work together in pairs or teams to engage in coding through simple apps and robotics such as Artie 3000, Dash or Dot from Wonder Workshop, Makeblock kits, and Lego BOOST. Introduce the robotics to children prior to use, and describe the ways in which the robot can be coded to move and engage with them.

Dot and Cubelet Robots

PROVOCATION 4: DIGITAL DOCUMENTATION

This provocation encourages children to use interactive media to document their learning in portfolio form; the documentation can be used in parent-teacher conferences. Interactive media includes technologies such as software programs, apps, electronic books, digital cameras, and video cameras. Children can also use tablets or digital cameras to record images of their work.

When given the opportunity, young children who participate in the documentation of their work and share their understandings with others take ownership of their thinking and have opportunities for reflective thinking. Young learners' engagement with interactive media for documentation should support playful learning, sustained explorations, and opportunities to share their understandings with others. Readily available documentation programs include the following:

- PowerPoint: a software package that allows for the creation of presentations through a series of slides

- Prezi: a cloud-based program available at https://prezi.com/

- Animoto: an online video-creation program available at https://animoto.com/

- Kizoa: an online program that supports the creation of slideshows, videos, and animated collages, available at https://www.kizoa.com/

- Google Sites: supports the creation of simple websites with custom templates, available at https://sites.google.com/new

To protect the images and children in your classroom, enable the privacy settings on whichever technology you use, and use a password for any online site.

CONTENT AND SKiLLS EXPERiENCED iN THiS PROVOCATiON

- **Technology:** use of digital tools to construct and communicate knowledge

- **Language arts and literacy:** writing

- **Creativity skills:** communication and collaboration, originality, elaboration

MATERiALS

- Computers or tablets

- Interactive software that supports the creation of documentation

PROVOCATiON PROMPT

How do others know what we are learning?

DiFFERENTiATiON BY GRADE LEVEL

- Pre-K and kindergarten students need simple websites or programs that allow them to navigate independently. Alternatively, encourage them to take photographs of the work they want to document, and then print those photographs so that children can add them to a paper-based portfolio. To build reflection and elaboration into the experience, provide time for the children to share their documentation with others. These discussions help children to better understand what they are learning and what they have come to know.

- First-, second-, and third-grade students can explore simple programs and apps that support documentation via slides, websites, or even videos. Find or create an initial guided exploration of the program or app for the children as they build their understanding of how to document their work using the new tool. As children gain proficiency in writing and reading, you can encourage them to add descriptive text to provide context and background information for the images they include in the documentation.

PROVOCATION 5: ELECTRONICS KIT EXPLORATIONS

Electronics kits designed for young learners help to support both interactive technology use and physical-science understandings of energy. A few examples of readily available electronics kits that young children can use independently include the following:

- Smart Circuits kits from SmartLab

- Snap Circuits from Elenco

- Circuit Cubes

- Makey Makey kits

In this provocation, electronics kits support children's hands-on creation of safe, simple circuits. A *circuit* is the path that an electric current travels. A simple circuit contains the three components necessary to have a functioning electric circuit: a source of voltage, a conductive path, and a resistor. When children create a functioning simple circuit, low voltage flows through the conductive path to a resistor, which "turns on" and does the work it was designed to do (a light turns on, an object turns, a sound comes through a speaker, and so on). Young children will find it helpful to work together in pairs or teams as they work through the trial-and-error process of circuit building.

CONTENT AND SKILLS EXPERIENCED IN THIS PROVOCATION

- **Technology:** use of digital tools to construct knowledge

- **Physical science:** energy, simple circuits

- **Creativity skills:** visualization, solution finding, strategic planning

MATERIALS

- Electronics kits

- Compatible batteries or power sources

- Defined workspaces to corral kit components for easy access

PROVOCATION PROMPT

What makes a light turn on [or whatever action the objects in your kit do when the circuit is complete]?

DIFFERENTIATION BY GRADE LEVEL

- Pre-K, kindergarten, and first-grade students will find simple, snap-together block circuits such as Circuit Cubes easiest to use, because they allow children to build functioning simple circuits without requiring a detailed read of instructions and steps. They can achieve movement or action through trial and error as they add new pieces, take away pieces, or rearrange pieces they've already placed.

- Second- and third-grade students can explore a variety of electronics kits. Many kits for children in these grades come with step-by-step instructions to build increasingly complex, multipart circuits. Encourage the children to think through the circuits they build as they move from simple to complex. They may need encouragement if they build a circuit that does not function on the first try. Taking it apart and rebuilding it strengthens the process of understanding and allows the children to see where they made a mistake.

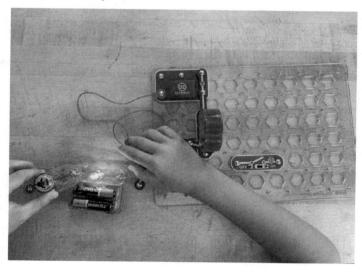

Snap Circuits explorations with a third-grade team

CHAPTER 3

ENGINEERING PROVOCATIONS

Engineering is often the least explored STEAM content area in many early childhood classrooms, with the exception of the block area found in pre-K or kindergarten classrooms. However, young learners express much interest in the processes of design, building, testing, and redesign during engineering experiences. It is for this reason that many school libraries have added small makerspaces, where children can come and freely explore a variety of building materials. The engineering provocations you'll find in this chapter use familiar materials—paper, blocks, Legos, and more—to engage children in aspects of engineering design. Because design and building take time, you'll want to assure your students that they can work on these provocations for numerous days. This means that you will need to consider where and how you can store their partially complete creations.

PROVOCATiON 1: KiNETiC SCULPTURE

Kinetic art refers to artwork that has movement that we can see and that is central to the piece. Examples of everyday kinetic art can include mobiles or even large pinwheels. These types of objects involve an *applied force*, which is a force exerted on an object by another object.

For this provocation, children will engage in an engineering design experience using readily available materials for construction and decoration to create kinetic sculptures. Showing printed images or videos of kinetic sculptures can inspire your students. Some well-known examples include Alexander Calder's colorful, geometric mobiles and David C. Roy's intricate wooden sculptures.

CONTENT AND SKiLLS EXPERiENCED iN THiS PROVOCATiON

- **Engineering:** engineering design, explorations of motion and applied force

- **Visual arts:** three-dimensional (3-D) sculpture making

- **Creativity skills:** visualization, solution finding, originality, strategic planning

MATERiALS

- Various small building materials (such as small blocks, Legos, cardboard, craft sticks, toothpicks, and chenille stems)

- Colored paper or cardboard (pre-K and kindergarten)

- Straws and connectors or wooden sets with nuts and bolts (first and second grades)

- Scissors

- Tape

- Glue

- String

PROVOCATiON PROMPTS

- Can you create shapes that will be fun to watch move on a mobile? (pre-K and kindergarten)

- Can you build a structure with a moving part?

DiFFERENTiATiON BY GRADE LEVEL

- Pre-K and kindergarten students benefit from creating kinetic objects that they have seen before, such as a mobile. A provocation for them might include creating organic (irregular) or geometric shapes out of colored paper or cardboard and then later working alongside you to affix the shapes to string and a center piece such as a craft stick.

- First- and second-grade students might benefit from a structured experience the first time they build a kinetic sculpture. Materials developed for building with interlocking pieces, such as straws and connectors or wooden sets with nuts and bolts, may help provide your students with a solid base to which to add a moveable component, such as string or chenille pipe cleaners.

- Third-grade students may wish to create large pieces, as this experience tends to invite the creation of objects that grow as the children add new materials and components. Be sure to have plenty of room for students to build and a place to store unfinished sculptures from day to day.

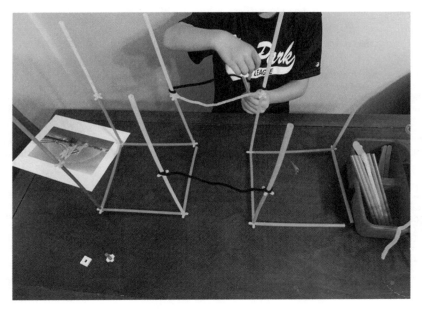

A second-grader creating a bridge structure with a walkway that sways

PROVOCATiON 2: DESIGN A CAR

Provocations that involve drawing plans and use design thinking encourage young learners to build their thinking, problem-solving, and creativity skills through playful engagement in tasks that build upon their real-world experiences. Young children will benefit from open-ended tasks that encourage them to build upon their prior knowledge, have a basis in real-life experiences, and have no one correct solution. In this provocation your students will be exploring an everyday object that is familiar to them—a car—and they will be invited to use their prior knowledge of cars to design their own. Using a familiar object such as a car provides them with an entry point into the design task because they can draw upon their own experiences while engaging their imaginations and creativity skills.

CONTENT AND SKiLLS EXPERiENCED iN THiS PROVOCATiON

- **Engineering:** design thinking, planning

- **Visual arts:** drawing

- **Creativity skills:** visualization, flexibility, originality, strategic planning

MATERiALS

- Scratch paper or engineering graph paper with a grid design

- Pencils, colored pencils, markers, or crayons

- Pictures of various cars

- Small toy cars

PROVOCATION PROMPT

What type of car will you design?

DIFFERENTIATION BY GRADE LEVEL

- Pre-K and kindergarten students will benefit from creating multiple sketches of their designs while they work out their ideas on paper. Encourage them to revise their sketches to make changes as they work.

- First-, second-, and third-grade students will enjoy comparing their designs with their peers, and a sharing experience may also give them ideas to help them revise their designs. This provocation can also be extended into a construction experience after the design phase by encouraging the students to bring their plans to life by using a variety of small building materials.

Pre-K student car designs

PROVOCATION 3: PAPER STRUCTURES

An important part of the engineering design cycle is creating *prototypes*, or models to test, which encourages children to put their ideas into a tangible form. As children gain more experience creating and making design or building plans, you can further their understanding of the purpose of making plans. Prototypes help an engineer think through their designs. Explain that design-based thinking is a process we can use to support our thinking and ideas in real time; we don't always have to have everything figured out or know the correct answer before we begin working. Your students will benefit from hearing that plans do not have to be perfect. The goal is to create a design plan to make our thoughts visible and help to guide us while we are creating. Encourage your students to see revision as a valuable and important part of the process and not as being wrong or having created their plan incorrectly. Revisions are a chance to think through new ideas. Repetition is an important part of the process of learning for young children. By encouraging your students to engage in redesign, you are helping them to strengthen their existing understanding and apply their previous knowledge to the current experience. A simple model of the engineering design process for young learners can involve the following steps:

- Asking a question

- Imagining a solution or design

- Making a plan

- Creating a product

- Improving through redesign

In this provocation, children can work through the design process as they ask a question and then imagine, plan, create, and redesign a 3-D paper structure.

CONTENT AND SKiLLS EXPERiENCED iN THiS PROVOCATiON

- **Engineering:** design-based thinking, planning

- **Visual arts:** creating 3-D sculptures

- **Creativity skills:** visualization, flexibility, originality, strategic planning

MATERiALS

- A variety of paper (such as paper scraps and paper of varying weights and thicknesses)

- Tape or glue

- Markers, paints, and crayons

- Pictures of both unique and familiar buildings

PROVOCATION PROMPTS

- What will your structure look like?

- What will your structure be used for?

DIFFERENTIATION BY GRADE LEVEL

This provocation is easily accessible for all students from pre-K through third grade. Younger students may need help from teachers or peers as they tape or glue parts of their structures. You can encourage older students to extend the experience by writing about their structures.

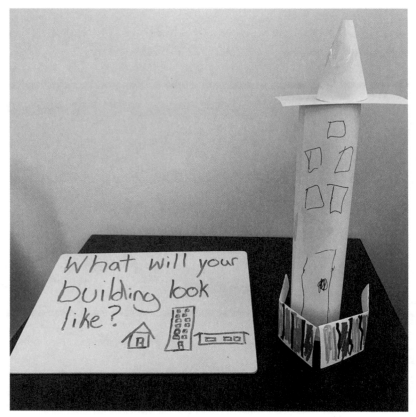

A first-grader's paper castle with a colorful fence

PROVOCATION 4: CLASSROOM REDESIGN

Reimagining and redesign are an important part of the engineering design process. In the classroom, however, young children are often given only enough time to create a singular product and do not have the opportunity to engage in redesign based upon what they learn or experience. This provocation encourages children to work in small teams to reimagine and redesign a familiar place—their classroom. You will want to ensure that your students understand that you may not be able to actually redesign the classroom they plan, but their design plans can help you to see what they find most valuable and interesting within a classroom. Inviting your students to share or display their plans can also help them to see that their work and ideas are valuable and meaningful.

CONTENT AND SKILLS EXPERIENCED IN THIS PROVOCATION

- **Engineering:** design-based thinking, planning

- **Visual arts:** drawing

- **Creativity skills:** visualization, flexibility, originality, communication and collaboration

MATERIALS

- Sketch paper

- Large sheets of paper

- Pencils

- Cut-out shapes to trace to represent classroom tables or other important objects

- Rulers to assist in drawing lines

PROVOCATION PROMPT

How could our classroom look?

DIFFERENTIATION BY GRADE LEVEL

This provocation is easily accessible for all students from pre-K through third grade. Encourage the teams to sketch their ideas on the sketch paper. They can trace shapes to represent furniture or other important objects in the classroom. Invite them to share their sketches with others and to revise as needed. Promote idea sharing within the classroom. When they are ready, encourage them to draw their final plans on large sheets of paper and to share them with others.

PROVOCATION 5: COMPETING ROBOTS

For young learners, active engagement with technology (rather than passive consumption of it) is a central idea related to understanding applications of technology and engineering. Active engagement supports opportunities for children to engage in innovative thinking through planning, design, and exploration with digital technologies. This provocation, which blends technology and engineering through play, will engage your students in a coding-design experience using simple robotics. Play-based experiences with coding allow young children to engage in mathematics and language skills, as well as a new way to solve problems, within a meaningful and engaging context. Coding with robotics involves logical and discrete steps to create observable robotic actions.

CONTENT AND SKILLS EXPERIENCED IN THIS PROVOCATION

- **Engineering:** design and planning with digital technologies

- **Technology:** engagement in innovative thinking through coding

- **Creativity skills:** visualization, strategic planning, solution finding

Provoking Curiosity

MATERIALS

- 2 Microbric Edison robots or other simple hobby programmable robots

- Pencils or dry-erase markers

- Paper or whiteboards

PROVOCATiON PROMPT

Can you program your robot to win?

DiFFERENTiATiON BY GRADE LEVEL

Programmable robots are best used with pre-K, kindergarten, and first-grade students under the close observation and support of an adult. These media often require children to have previous experiences with robotics in order to work independently or alongside other students. If your young students are new to programmable robotics, you will want to take the time to introduce the information and build the students' knowledge of and experience with the robots prior to encouraging independent explorations. For children with prior experience and for older students, this provocation could follow a simple introduction, as the programmable robots will come with suggestions and instructions that you can encourage children to explore and use to support their interactions. Encourage the children to work in teams as they program their robots to compete against each other in doing simple tasks or races.

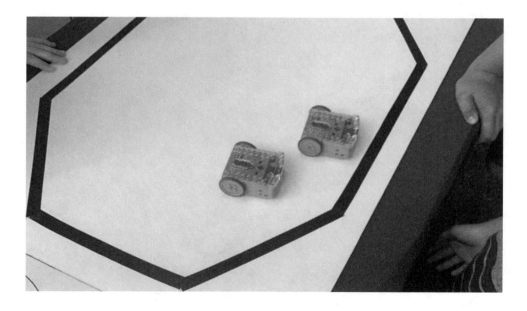

CHAPTER 4

ARTS
PROVOCATIONS

The A in STEAM represents both visual and performing arts. Engaging young children in art-making, music, movement, and drama experiences has been a traditional and beloved part of early childhood education. When the arts are a central part of STEM learning, children have valuable opportunities to use their creativity skills and knowledge of the arts to increase the development of STEM-focused content understanding. Arts-rich STEM learning can also help to provide children with a comfortable entry point into their STEM learning, as you encourage them to draw, write, sing, or dance their ideas. Many provocations throughout this book and in this chapter integrate visual and performing opportunities with STEM content in a truly meaningful way. The arts are a central part of children's explorations, learning, and documentation.

PROVOCATION 1: EXPLORING COLOR

Understanding color and how to create color is an important part of early visual-arts experiences. Through exploration experiences with color, children can begin to understand the relationships between colors and how to mix them to develop a specific color combination.

In this provocation, children will explore colors by recreating a chosen color using watercolor paints or chalk pastels. These two art media offer the best possibilities to support children's mixing and layering of colors. Paint-sample swatches form the basis for this provocation and are available at most home-supply stores. Choosing a wide range of swatches will ensure that children have interesting choices for exploration.

CONTENT AND SKILLS EXPERIENCED IN THIS PROVOCATION

- **Visual arts:** exploring color
- **Creativity skills:** visualization, flexibility

MATERIALS

- Paint-sample swatches
- Chalk pastels or watercolor paints and water with small paintbrushes
- Color wheel to help children visualize the colors prior to mixing and layering

PROVOCATION PROMPT

Can you create a color match?

DIFFERENTIATION BY GRADE LEVEL

- Pre-K and kindergartners can explore the three primary colors (red, yellow, and blue) and the three secondary colors (orange, green, and violet).

- First-graders can explore primary colors, secondary colors, and the six tertiary colors (red-orange, yellow-orange, yellow-green, blue-green, blue-violet, red-violet), which are formed by mixing a primary color with a secondary color.

- Second- and third-graders can explore primary, secondary, and tertiary colors and also explore tint (a mixture of pure colors with only white added) and tone (a mixture of pure colors with only dark gray added).

Creating a color match: exploring tint

PROVOCATION 2: THINKING THROUGH DRAWING

Drawing can serve as a communication tool for young children as well as a creative way to express their feelings and thoughts. There are several different categories of drawing that can be a part of STEAM experiences for young learners.

- *Observational drawing* encourages children to draw what they see—such as the shape of a leaf or the movement of a butterfly.

- *Emotive drawing* explores the expression of different emotions, feelings, and moods.

- Sketches are often a part of *analytic drawing*, which is similar to observational drawing but focuses on a small part of something and is created to communicate a clear idea or understanding of that part.

- *Geometric drawing* typically involves creating an image with measured dimensions and is used as a precursor to building or creating an object or sculpture.

- *Exploratory drawings* let the artist play with ideas, explore ways of representing them, and use lines in novel ways.

For this experience, children will engage in exploratory drawing with open-ended drawing starters. Drawing starters can be incomplete designs you create for the children. With drawing starters, children are encouraged to add to the incomplete drawing in front of them.

Remember that the arts media you provide can support children's drawing experiences or can provide unexpected challenges. For example, drawing with thick-tipped markers can be challenging, as they make it difficult for younger children to control the degree of detail they can add to their drawings.

CONTENT AND SKILLS EXPERIENCED IN THIS PROVOCATION

- **Visual arts:** drawing

- **Creativity skills:** visualization, originality

MATERIALS

- Drawing starters

- Pencils, colored pencils, fine-tipped markers, crayons, or oil pastels

PROVOCATION PROMPTS

- What can you add to this drawing?

- What can you turn this image into?

DIFFERENTIATION BY GRADE LEVEL

This provocation is easily accessible for all students from pre-K through third grade, because you can vary the complexity of the drawing starters to meet the needs, skills, and interests of your students.

Examples of simple drawing starters

PROVOCATiON 3: PAiNTiNG ON EARTH MATERiALS

Children are most often given paper to paint on, but the addition of unconventional painting surfaces can enliven their painting experiences and pose new challenges due to uneven surfaces and varying textures. Unconventional earth materials for children to paint on can include leaves, seeds, seashells, sticks, and rocks. This provocation will invite children to create designs and images and to explore the ways they can use paint to decorate a unique, often uneven, or rough surface.

CONTENT AND SKiLLS EXPERiENCED iN THiS PROVOCATiON

- **Visual arts:** painting

- **Earth science:** materials exploration

- **Creativity skills:** visualization, originality

MATERiALS

- Earth materials, such as leaves, shells, seeds, sticks, and rocks

- Washable tempera paint

- Paintbrushes

- Paper cups filled with water

- Paper towels

PROVOCATiON PROMPTS

- What will it feel like to paint a leaf [seed, seashell, stick, rock, or whichever earth materials you have chosen]?

- What shapes can you fit onto a single leaf? (first through third grade)

- Can you paint an insect on a rock? (first through third grade)

DIFFERENTIATION BY GRADE LEVEL

- Pre-K and kindergartners will benefit from an exploratory experience that uses a variety of similar objects but still offers opportunities for choice if they are new to selecting their own materials. For example, providing a selection of rocks of various sizes, shapes, and colors offers children the choice of choosing a rock without overwhelming them by including a wider selection of earth materials. This way they can focus on the experience of painting without being overwhelmed by materials choices.

- First-, second-, and third-graders can have the same kind of exploratory experience, but you can also create additional challenges by inviting them to create specific images or designs on their materials. You can link classroom science or math topics to the provocation with invitations that address the content they are learning.

Third-graders painting insects on rocks

PROVOCATION 4: PLANETARY EXPLORATION

From popular-culture books and movies to the nightly news, young children are introduced to different understandings of the planets beyond Earth. A practical explanation of our solar system is that it is made up of the sun and all the objects—planets, asteroids, and other things—that orbit around it. Our sun is a star with a strong gravitational pull; planets and other objects are pulled into orbit around the sun because of this. There are eight planets in our solar system. Their order is, from closest to farthest from the sun, Mercury, Venus, Earth, Mars, Jupiter, Saturn, Uranus, and Neptune. The four closest to the sun are called *terrestrial planets* because they are primarily made up of rock and metal and are mostly solid. The four planets farthest from the sun are much larger than the terrestrial planets and are mostly made up of gas. The differences in the colors of the planets are due to what they are made of and how their surfaces or atmospheres reflect and absorb sunlight. For example, the planet Mars is covered with a fine dust that contains iron oxide and gives Mars its orange color.

In this provocation, children will explore images and basic facts regarding the sizes and colors of the planets. This provocation can provide children with opportunities to further strengthen their understandings of concepts you've introduced during formal instructional time. When the whole class is learning about the planets and the reasons for their sizes and colors, use this provocation to help the children tap into what they are learning. With this knowledge, the children will be able to create a visual representation of an existing planet or a planet they imagine.

CONTENT AND SKILLS EXPERIENCED IN THIS PROVOCATION

- **Visual arts:** design and color explorations

- **Earth and space science:** solar system, planets

- **Creativity skills:** visualization, solution finding, communication and collaboration

MATERIALS

- Color images of the planets or access to virtual images via a tablet or computer

- Printed planet facts

- Paper

- Crayons, colored pencils, tempera paints, paintbrushes

PROVOCATION PROMPT

Why are the planets different sizes and colors?

DIFFERENTIATION BY GRADE LEVEL

Pre-K and kindergarten students will enjoy exploring the planetary images prior to choosing a planet as the subject of their artwork. Read the prompt to the children, and encourage them to draw or sketch their selected planet prior to beginning to add color.

For first-, second-, and third-graders, the provocation can involve a higher level of factual details and color explorations. Be sure to encourage them to notice the details in the color variations of each image in order to connect to the science behind the reasons the planets vary in size and color.

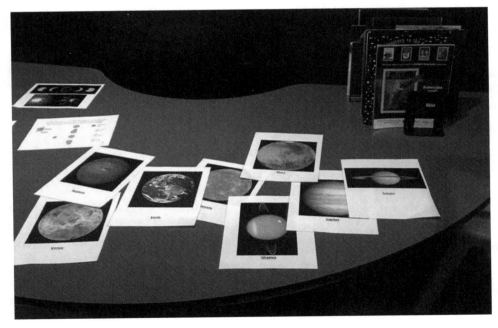

Planetary exploration

PROVOCATION 5: A STORY IN FOUR PICTURES

The visual arts can be used to facilitate story creation and storytelling. Many cultures from around the globe use images for storytelling. For instance, *kamishibai* storytelling from Japan uses beautifully illustrated cards, and *Kavad Katha* storytelling from India uses 3-D storytelling boxes that open to show detailed pictures.

This provocation invites children to develop a storyline and create images to tell the story without words. This experience will help children to better understand how images alone can be used to communicate information and share ideas and emotions with others.

CONTENT AND SKILLS EXPERIENCED IN THIS PROVOCATION

- **Visual arts:** emotive and analytic drawing for storytelling

- **Creativity skills:** visualization, communication, strategic planning, originality

MATERIALS

- Sheets of paper with two to four individual blocks of equal space

- Drawing arts media (such as pencils, colored pencils, markers, and crayons)

PROVOCATION PROMPT

- What story can you tell with four pictures? (pre-K through third grade)

- Pre-K and kindergarten:

    » "My favorite game to play is . . . "

    » "My friend and I play . . . "

    » "My favorite pet is . . . "

DiFFERENTiATiON BY GRADE LEVEL

- To support the development of their storylines, provide pre-K and kindergarten students with simple storytelling prompts connected to their daily experiences, such as "My favorite game to play is . . . ," "My friend and I play . . . ," or "My favorite pet is . . ." You may want to introduce this provocation with papers that have only two boxes so that the children gain experience with visual storytelling without being concerned with filling in more story boxes. As they gain experience with the task, you can increase the number of story boxes to match their growing storytelling skills.

- First-, second-, and third-graders can also use storytelling prompts, but they may enjoy the open-ended nature of creating a story about anything they are interested in exploring visually. To extend the communication aspect of the experience, encourage children to use the images they create to share their stories with others.

PROVOCATiON 6: SEEDS, FRUiTS, AND VEGETABLES

The integration of science and visual-arts learning is a natural pairing because both content areas require students to closely observe and document their observations. Life-science content for young learners is focused on understanding the parts of a plant, plant needs, and plant growth. This provocation will encourage students to connect their understandings of plants and growth to the visual arts as they create a drawing or painting of a fruit or vegetable that grows from seeds. Provide seeds from fruits or vegetables for exploration and inspiration. As your students will be handling seeds in this provocation, be aware of any student allergies or other concerns with seed size when choosing the seeds for exploration.

CONTENT AND SKiLLS EXPERiENCED iN THiS PROVOCATiON

- **Visual art:** creating representational drawing/paintings

- **Life science:** plants and plant growth

- **Creativity skills:** visualization, exploration, and communication

MATERIALS

- Seeds of varying sizes (such as those from grapes, apples, oranges, small pumpkins or gourds, tomatoes, eggplants, cucumbers, pomegranates, strawberries, and avocados)

- Images of the fruits or vegetables associated with the available seeds

- Paper

- Paintbrushes

- Arts media (such as crayons, colored pencils, and tempera paints)

PROVOCATION PROMPT

Which seed grows your favorite fruit or vegetable?

DIFFERENTIATION BY GRADE LEVEL

This provocation is easily accessible for all students. They will enjoy the opportunity to explore the various seeds and the related images prior to creating an image of their favorite.

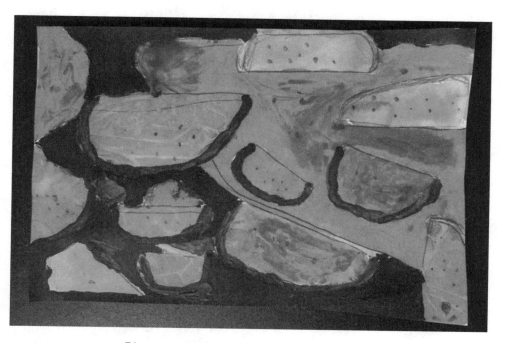

Plants and seeds visual-arts provocation

CHAPTER 5

MATHEMATICS PROVOCATIONS

Mathematics is often thought of as a core thread tying the STEAM disciplines together, which underscores the necessity for young learners to build a solid mathematical foundation in the early years. Integrative mathematics experiences, which bring math together with one or more of the other STEAM disciplines, can help to build a foundation in math while also helping children to see math as connected to their everyday experiences. The mathematics provocations in this chapter emphasize children's hands-on, minds-on learning through direct interactions with mathematics manipulatives as they work alongside their peers. Mathematics provocations can provide children with opportunities to further strengthen their understandings of the mathematics concepts you've introduced during formal instructional time.

PROVOCATiON 1: DiCE GAMES

Exploring numbers through gameplay provides young learners with opportunities to build upon and strengthen the understandings they develop during planned mathematics lessons in your classroom. Children in classrooms from pre-K through third grade need opportunities to develop and apply quantification skills in order to deepen their knowledge of numbers and the relationships between numbers. *Quantification*—determining or expressing the quantity of a group of objects—can be developed by engaging in playful mathematics experiences centered on creating object sets and adding to, subtracting from, multiplying by, and dividing the sets. In this provocation your students will be working together to play simple dice games to strengthen their understanding of and fluency with numbers.

CONTENT AND SKiLLS EXPERiENCED iN THiS PROVOCATiON

- **Mathematics:** number, number sense

- **Creativity skills:** solution finding, fluency, problem solving

MATERiALS

- Traditional six-sided cube dice

- Polyhedral dice with numerals on each face

- Counting chips (pre-K and kindergarten)

- Whiteboards

- Dry-erase markers

- Trays or small containers to keep rolled dice from escaping

PROVOCATION PROMPT

In this provocation, your prompt will change based upon the game you've introduced to the children. Examples of appropriate prompts include the following:

- Can you find the sum?

- What does it mean to round up?

- Can you make a number match?

Here are some simple dice games you can introduce to your students:

- **Adding Together:** Children can play this game with a partner or by themselves. If playing with a partner, each child rolls two traditional dice, adds the resulting numbers together, and finds the number that matches that sum on a polyhedral die. Whoever has the larger sum wins the round.

- **Rounding Up/Rounding Down:** Each child rolls two traditional dice (one at a time) and writes down each rolled number. The first number rolled becomes the tens digit, and the second number rolled becomes the ones digit of a new number (for example, 5 + 6 turns into 56). The child then rounds his number up or down to the nearest multiple of ten (for instance, 56 becomes 60). The child with the larger number wins.

- **Race to 100:** Rolling one traditional die at a time, two children race to see who can roll a total of 100 first. The child writes down the number she rolls on each turn and adds the numbers together as she goes, to keep track of the sum.

- **Number Match:** A child rolls a polyhedral die. The child writes down the result and then rolls a traditional die to see if she can match the number on the polyhedral die. She continues rolling the traditional die until she rolls a match.

DIFFERENTIATION BY GRADE LEVEL

- Pre-K and kindergarten students can play very simple games, such as Adding Together and Number Match. They can use counting chips to help them add the numbers.

- First- and second-graders can play more collaborative and more complicated games, such as Rounding Up/Rounding Down and Race to 100.

- Third-graders can work with partners to play these suggested games but will also enjoy the challenge of creating their own math games. Encourage each pair of children to share their game with others.

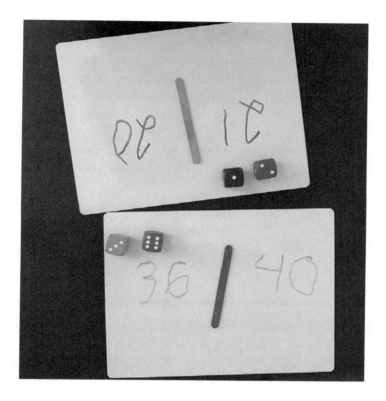

Second-graders playing Rounding Up/Rounding Down

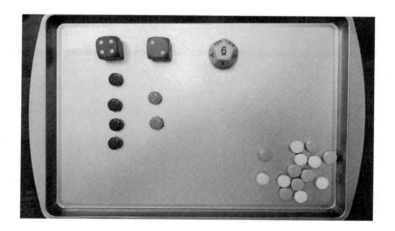

Kindergartner playing Adding Together with counting chips

PROVOCATION 2: CREATE 3-D SHAPE CHARACTERS

Shapes, geometry, and spatial sense are important aspects of early mathematics experiences. Throughout the early childhood years, children build their understanding of 2-D and 3-D shapes and the many configurations of those shapes in the world around them by actively exploring concepts of shape, size, position, directionality, and motion. Through active engagement in exploring these concepts of shapes and spatial awareness, children build flexible visual-reasoning skills, concepts of shapes and spatial awareness, and understanding of the attributes of geometric figures.

In this provocation, children will make 3-D shapes and use them to construct a 3-D character. You may want to encourage the children to build their characters inside shallow trays so that they can easily set them aside to dry. Providing pictures or drawings of 3-D shapes helps to remind the children of the many different shapes they can create.

CONTENT AND SKILLS EXPERIENCED IN THIS PROVOCATION

- **Mathematics:** geometry, spatial awareness

- **Creativity skills:** visualization, flexibility, strategic planning, originality

MATERIALS

- Flexible modeling material (such as clay, playdough, or Model Magic)

- Scratch paper

- Pencils

- Shallow trays (optional)

- Pictures or drawings of 3-D shapes (such as a sphere, cylinder, cone, cube, cuboid, triangular pyramid, square pyramid, and triangular prism)

PROVOCATiON PROMPTS

- What shapes will your character contain?

- Can you create a character using at least five 3-D shapes? (third grade)

- Can you create a character with cylinders and spheres? (third grade)

DiFFERENTiATiON BY GRADE LEVEL

- Pre-K and kindergarten students can work with partners to build a collaborative character. Working with a partner provides an extra set of hands during the building phase, which can help to provide stability and support. Including pictures or drawing of 3-D shapes will help to remind the children of the many different shapes they can create.

- First- and second-graders often find it helpful to create a plan or a sketch of their character before they begin building, because planning gives them a chance to think through their decisions before working to construct them.

- Third-graders will enjoy working on a challenge that asks them to attempt to include either specific 3-D shapes or a certain number of 3-D shapes in their work.

Kindergartners working on a collaborative 3-D character

PROVOCATiON 3: PERFECT SYMMETRY iN NATURE

Young children use geometric motions naturally when they manipulate loose parts and various materials to turn, flip, and slide each piece into place. *Symmetry* is the geometric quality of being made up of identical parts facing each other across an axis or line, creating a mirror image. Children can transfer this understanding to an understanding of shape when they observe that a square block has four equal sides or that a piece of paper cut into a circle can be folded down the center to create a half circle.

In this provocation experience, children will create temporary, moveable mirror images with various loose parts.

CONTENT AND SKiLLS EXPERiENCED iN THiS PROVOCATiON

- **Mathematics:** geometry, symmetry

- **Creativity skills:** visualization, flexibility, strategic planning, originality

MATERiALS

- Various loose parts (such as small glass or plastic cabochons, small paper or plastic shapes, buttons, small colorful stones, pompoms, and small beads)

- Paper or dry-erase boards with lines of symmetry drawn down the center

PROVOCATiON PROMPT

Can you create a symmetrical design?

DiFFERENTiATiON BY GRADE LEVEL

- Pre-K and kindergarten students can work with partners to create symmetrical shapes. Working with a partner also helps the children check their work as they cooperate to place materials.

- First-, second-, and third-graders will enjoy working on a challenge that invites them to connect symmetrical design back to the life-science content they are exploring. For example, students could find symmetry in nature—such as butterfly wings or leaves—and could re-create those designs or create new ones based upon their observations of the natural world.

A first-grader's symmetrical design

PROVOCATION 4: PATTERNING WITH NONTRADITIONAL MATERIALS

Patterning involves the recognition of existing relationships between objects. Patterning is a fundamental mathematical understanding that serves as the cornerstone of algebraic thinking. Patterning skills for students from pre-K through third grade include being able to recognize, extend, create, and copy patterns. Children can use patterns to predict or explain the relationships between objects.

The simplest pattern to introduce to preschool and kindergarten children is known as an AB, AB pattern. For example, colored buttons lined up as red, blue, red, blue are an example of an AB, AB pattern. More complex patterns for first- through third-graders can include ABC, ABC; AABB, AABB; and ABCD, ABCD patterns. In this provocation, children will create patterns with a variety of materials—the more variety in materials choices, the more challenging the task. Inviting the students to label their patterns after creating them provides an internal check of their work.

CONTENT AND SKILLS EXPERIENCED IN THIS PROVOCATION

- **Mathematics:** geometry, patterning
- **Creativity skills:** visualization, strategic planning, originality

MATERIALS

- Traditional math manipulatives (such as counting bears, colored counting disks, or small plastic shapes)

- Loose parts (such as small glass or plastic cabochons, small paper or plastic shapes, buttons, small colorful stones, seashells, leaves, small sticks, pompoms, and small beads)

- Paper or whiteboards

- Pencils or dry-erase markers

PROVOCATION PROMPT

What pattern will you create?

DIFFERENTIATION BY GRADE LEVEL

- Pre-K and kindergarten students may find it helpful to use math manipulatives to create simple pattern strings.

- First-, second-, and third-graders will enjoy the challenge of patterning with nontraditional, loose-parts materials. Encourage them to create a variety of pattern strings and to label the patterns below the placed materials to check their work.

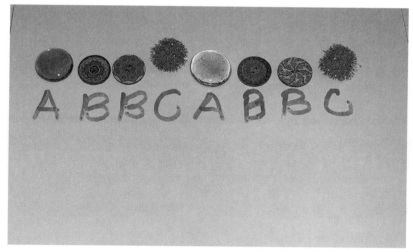

A second-grader's ABBC, ABBC pattern string

PROVOCATiON 5: MATCHiNG 3-D SHAPES

Connecting 2-D and 3-D understandings is a challenging task for many young children. Exploratory experiences with manipulating 3-D shapes can help children make connections among 2-D and 3-D shapes. Three-dimensional shapes are solid or hollow and have length, width, and height. Common 3-D shapes include the following:

- Sphere
- Cylinder
- Cone
- Cube

- Cuboid
- Triangular pyramid
- Square pyramid
- Triangular prism

In this provocation, children will create 3-D shapes or matching 2-D and 3-D shape sides, depending on their knowledge and experience with shapes.

CONTENT AND SKiLLS EXPERiENCED iN THiS PROVOCATiON

- **Mathematics:** geometry
- **Creativity skills:** visualization, flexibility

MATERiALS

- Modeling material (such as clay, playdough, or Model Magic)
- 3-D shape models or images for reference
- 2-D shape outlines (first and second grade)

PROVOCATION PROMPTS

· What 3-D shapes can you make?

· Can you create 3-D shapes to match 2-D outlines? (first and second grade)

· Can you create two or three 3-D shapes that share a side? (third grade)

DIFFERENTIATION BY GRADE LEVEL

· Pre-K and kindergarten students can create 3-D shapes but will need to use shape models or pictures to guide their work.

· First- and second-graders can create 3-D shapes and match them to 2-D outlines of shapes (for instance, placing a cube on top of a square).

· Third-graders will enjoy working on a challenge that asks them to find similarities among 3-D shapes, such as creating 3-D shapes that share a side.

Third-graders working on matching 3-D shapes

PROVOCATiON 6: HELPiNG HANDS

Addition is combining two or more groups of numbers to discover the total. *Subtraction* is taking away one number from another number to discover how many are left. Addition and subtraction are *inverse operations* because one operation can undo the other operation. For example, adding six and two to get eight can be undone by subtracting two from eight, which leaves six. Teaching inverse operations together helps children to understand the relationships among numbers, operations, and fact families.

A *fact family* is a group of mathematical facts that use the same numbers. For instance, a fact family with two, four, and six might look like this: $2 + 4 = 6$, $4 + 2 = 6$, $6 - 4 = 2$, and $6 - 2 = 4$. You can reinforce children's understanding of fact families to help them learn or strengthen the connection between addition and subtraction and to help them gain fluency with basic addition and subtraction facts.

When young children are working independently with addition and subtraction concepts, you can best support them by providing opportunities to learn through hands-on experiences with countable objects or place-value blocks. Once children demonstrate flexible, robust understanding of addition, subtraction, and basic fact families, you can introduce multiplication in a playful, hands-on manner. Introducing multiplication as repeated addition helps young learners to connect their established understanding to the new understanding. For instance, multiplying 5 by 3 will provide the same answer as adding $5 + 5 + 5$.

In this provocation, your students will work to solve a variety of mathematics challenges using the support of the helping hands to guide their work. A *helping hand* is made from a disposable glove filled with sand and then sealed. The number of hands each child will need depends upon the details of the provocation experience.

CONTENT AND SKiLLS EXPERiENCED iN THiS PROVOCATiON

- **Mathematics:** addition, subtraction, multiplication

- **Creativity skills:** solution finding, fluency, flexibility, problem solving

MATERIALS

- Disposable gloves

- Sand

- Paper or small whiteboards

- Pencil or dry-erase markers

- Counting objects (such as colored counters, craft sticks, counting bears, small beads, or buttons)

PROVOCATiON PROMPTS

- Do you need an extra hand for addition and subtraction? (pre-K, kindergarten, first and second grades)

- Do you need an extra hand for multiplication? (third grade)

DiFFERENTiATiON BY GRADE LEVEL

- Encourage pre-K and kindergarten students to solve simple addition and subtraction problems. You can extend the work they do during math lessons by writing problems using the numbers you have previously introduced.

- First- and second-graders can work on addition and subtraction problems or explore simple fact families by using multiple helping hands.

- Third-graders can explore multiplication using multiple helping hands and written problems that connect multiplication to repeated addition.

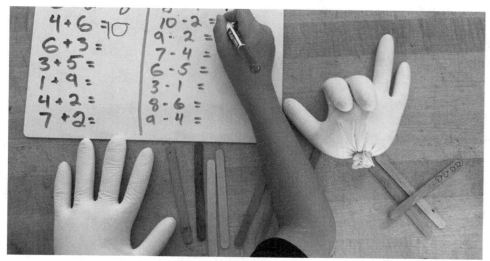

A first-grader adding and subtracting with a pair of helping hands

CHAPTER 6

CLASSROOM STEAM MAKERSPACES FOR OPEN-ENDED AND ONGOING PROVOCATIONS

This final chapter includes ideas for creating STEAM makerspaces that are accessible for young children using materials you probably already have in your classroom. A makerspace presents easy-to-access materials that promote natural provocations for inquiry, exploration, and creation. Makerspaces within early childhood classrooms can provide a long-term physical space for children to build and create. These spaces provide opportunities for children to turn their ideas into actions. A STEAM makerspace is an inviting area of the classroom with carefully selected materials, all of which support inquiry into the STEAM disciplines—materials that children can use in countless ways. STEAM makerspaces provide a vehicle for open-ended provocations, a necessary balance to the more specific STEAM provocations presented in the previous chapters.

BENEFITS OF CLASSROOM MAKERSPACES

A makerspace provides a stimulating learning experience within a collaborative working area, where children can do the following:

- Think, create, share, and make decisions

- Engage in hands-on, minds-on, student-led learning

- Use familiar and accessible materials in new and unexpected ways

- Work alongside or collaboratively with peers

- Tackle problems and develop solutions to test and revise

- Find the natural connections that exist among STEAM disciplines

Countless benefits abound when children have the opportunity to explore in a makerspace. They can develop unique skills based upon their engagement with various tools and materials, become more independent by making decisions to guide their actions, build on their personal interests, and gain inspiration and encouragement to try new things within a flexible makerspace environment. As with the STEAM provocations presented in previous chapters, children can engage in planning and design work during makerspace provocations by creating sketches, drawings, or physical models. These representations are useful to explore ideas for overcoming a challenge or developing a new idea. Makerspaces in an early childhood classroom can involve materials that range from low-tech to more advanced media. Low-tech makerspaces use materials you probably already have on hand in your classroom, such as Legos, small blocks, magnetic tiles, Tinkertoys, K'Nex, Straw Builders, and other building toys. These spaces also allow children to join in without needing prior knowledge or experience to get started. Mixing more than one type of building toy into your makerspace will pose more challenges for your students and allow for a wider variety of constructions. Medium-tech makerspaces involve more specialized materials that will require children to have prior experience with the media or tools used. More specialized materials include digital media such as robotics and electronics kits.

CONTENT AND SKILLS EXPERIENCED IN MAKERSPACE PROVOCATIONS

- **Creativity skills:** visualization, communication and collaboration, solution finding, flexibility, elaboration, originality, problem solving, strategic planning

PROVOCATION PROMPT

What will you explore and create today?

TOOLS AND MATERIALS FOR CLASSROOM MAKERSPACES

As you plan for incorporating a STEAM makerspace into your classroom, consider the types of activities that children could engage in there. A possible range of activities might include the following:

- Construction or building

- Woodworking

- Tinkering with electronics and robotics

- Creating and testing models

- Creative art making

Designing a space to accommodate such a wide range of activities is a challenging process and will require you to carefully select materials that your students will be able to use in multiple ways. The following lists suggest a wide variety of materials that you could include in your STEAM makerspace. It is important to choose materials based upon the types of STEAM actions and content that you hope to inspire while also taking care to ensure that the materials you've selected are appropriate and safe for your students. Not all materials need to be included at any given time. Carefully observe the children's actions in the space to determine when to add, remove, or introduce new materials.

SAFETY EQUIPMENT AND TOOLS FOR MAKERSPACES

- Child-sized safety goggles
- Aprons or smocks
- Magnifying glasses
- Scissors
- Rulers
- Measuring tape
- Flashlights

- STEAM journals
- Timers
- Paintbrushes
- Markers
- Colored pencils
- Scales
- Child-sized tools (such as hammers, screwdrivers, and pliers)

SAFETY NOTE

Take care to ensure that your students know how to use any tools you provide in the makerspace. Simple demonstrations serve to explain how to use a tool and why we use a tool in such a manner. You will also need to ensure that you are following your school and state regulations for acceptable materials, media, and tools.

POSSIBLE MAKERSPACE MATERIALS

- Cardboard of varying sizes
- Tape (duct tape, Scotch tape, and masking tape)
- Blocks, Legos, or other building pieces of varying sizes
- Bottle caps
- Straws
- Cardboard tubes
- Recycled containers and bottles
- Packaging products (such as bubble wrap, foam peanuts, wrapping-paper scraps, cardboard, and Styrofoam inserts)
- Recycled spools and wheels from thread and ribbon
- Plastic cups and lids
- Corks
- Rubber bands
- Paper scraps
- Fabric remnants
- Silk scarves
- Ribbons

- Glass cabochons
- Mosaic tiles
- Rope and similar materials (such as yarn, embroidery thread, twine, and string)
- Bowls, containers, and baking tins
- Kitchen utensils (such as spoons, forks, potato mashers, hand mixers, and scoops)
- Funnels
- Paper clips
- Beads
- Pompoms
- Chenille stems
- Small balls
- Marbles
- Napkin rings
- Wood scraps
- Nuts, washers, and bolts
- Wire pieces of varying lengths (make sure there are no sharp ends)

- Small ceramic tiles
- Magnets
- Wooden dowel pieces of varying sizes
- PVC pipe pieces
- Paint-sample cards
- Rocks in a variety of sizes and textures
- Leaves
- Fresh and dried flowers
- Pinecones
- Seeds, dried beans, pods, acorns
- Sea glass
- Sticks of varying sizes
- Shells
- Feathers
- Electronics or robotics kits
- Broken electronics that can be taken apart

USING YOUR MAKERSPACE

During STEAM makerspace experiences, teachers should not direct children to create specific products or engage in prescribed explorations. Children should negotiate their own experiences and determine their own actions, with teacher guidance coming from the selection of materials for the space. Young children can sometimes be overwhelmed by the many materials offered in a makerspace, so you may find it helpful to provide initial provocation questions or suggestions to get them started. For example, a construction makerspace with a variety of blocks can also include images of a few different block structures along with a provocation prompt such as "Can you build a match?" The simple prompt can help a child get started and focus her time in the space. This can be especially helpful for children new to a classroom makerspace.

A simple provocation to help children focus in this makerspace

As in the Build a Shape Match makerspace, you will find it helpful to carefully select, display, and store makerspace materials so that they do not take over your classroom. Displaying materials in baskets or small containers for student use will help children to see all the materials available to them and will also provide a logical scaffold to help them to keep the area organized as they put away materials in their designated containers. A few steps to keep makerspaces organized and manageable in a classroom include the following:

- Keep an inventory of materials you have so that you know when to replenish supplies.

- Develop a list of a few loose materials that you would like to add to the space.

- Limit the amount and number of materials available in the area so that children are not overwhelmed.

The focus of the makerspace will change as you add or remove materials. Families can be a great source of help if you take the time to request recycled or excess materials—just be specific on the types of materials you are hoping to add so that the donations match up to the interests of the children and your safety requirements.

A preschooler constructing a house after
drawing a plan in a STEAM makerspace

REFERENCES AND RECOMMENDED READING

Bybee, Rodger, et al. 2006. *The BSCS 5E Instructional Model: Origins, Effectiveness, and Applications.* Report. Colorado Springs, CO: BSCS. http://www.fremonths. org/ourpages/auto/2008/5/11/1210522036057/bscs5efullreport2006.pdf

Dewey, John. 1916. *Democracy and Education.* New York, NY: The Free Press.

Dewey, John. 1902. *The Child and the Curriculum.* Chicago, IL: The University of Chicago Press.

Dewey, John. 1938. *Experience and Education.* New York, NY: Macmillan.

Gandini, Lella, et al., eds. 2005. *In the Spirit of the Studio: Learning from the Atelier of Reggio Emilia.* New York, NY: Teachers College Press.

Gandini, Lella. 2011. "Play and the Hundred Languages of Children." *American Journal of Play* 4(1): 1–18. http://www.journalofplay.org/sites/www.journalofplay.org/files/ pdf-articles/4-1-interview-gandini.pdf

Kolb, David. 1984. *Experiential Learning: Experience as the Source of Learning and Development.* Englewood Cliffs, NJ: Prentice-Hall.

Montessori, Maria. 1964. *The Absorbent Mind.* Wheaton, IL: Theosophical Press.

Pramling Samuelsson, Ingrid, Sonja Sheridan, and Pia Williams. 2006. "Five Preschool Curricula—Comparative Perspective." *International Journal of Early Childhood* 38(1): 11–30.

Vygotsky, Lev. 1962. *Thought and Language.* Edited and translated by Eugenia Hanfmann and Gertrude Vakar. Cambridge, MA: MIT Press.

INDEX

Provoking Curiosity